ALSO BY
Paul Durcan

THE ART OF LIFE

Paul Durcan

THE ART OF LIFE

Harvill *Secker*
LONDON

Published by HARVILL SECKER 2012

2 4 6 8 10 9 7 5 3 1

First published in Great Britain in 2004 by The Harvill Press

HARVILL SECKER
Random House
20 Vauxhall Bridge Road
London SW1V 2SA

www.vintage-books.co.uk

Addresses for companies within The Random House Group Limited can be
found at: www.randomhouse.co.uk/offices.htm

The Random House Group Limited Reg. No. 954009

A CIP catalogue record for this book is available from the British Library

ISBN 9781846557521 (trade paperback)

The Random House Group Limited supports The Forest Stewardship Council
(FSC®), the leading international forest certification organisation. Our books
carrying the FSC label are printed on FSC® certified paper. FSC is the only
forest certification scheme endorsed by the leading environmental organisations,
including Greenpeace. Our paper procurement policy can be found at
www.randomhouse.co.uk/environment

Typeset in Bembo by Palimpsest Book Production Limited,
Falkirk, Stirlingshire

Printed and bound in Great Britain by
MPG Books Ltd, Bodmin

TO
PATRICK O' BRIEN

sea light

and

ROSIE JOYCE
KITTY AMELIA JOYCE
and
BEATRICE DRUMMOND

night fishing

ACKNOWLEDGEMENTS

Versions of three of these poems were published in *Riposte*, the *Irish Times* and the *Sunday Independent*.

CONTENTS

THE ART OF LIFE

Golden Island Shopping Centre

After tortellini in The Olive Grove on the quays
I drive over to the adjacent shopping centre,
Golden Island Shopping Centre,
Around whose acres of car park
I drive in circles for quarter of an hour
Before finding a slot in a space painted yellow:
GOLDEN ISLAND EXPECTANT MOTHERS

Two hours later I stumble from Tesco
With high-altitude sickness;
Dazed, exhausted, apprehensive, breathless;
In worse condition than
Many a climber on the South Col of Everest.
Such mobs of shoppers on a Sunday afternoon,
Such powerlessness.

Loading up the boot of my car
I see through a white mist
A small, bejowled, red-headed, middle-aged lady in black
Standing in front of my car
With a Jack Russell terrier in a muzzle.
She is writing down my registration number.

I inquire: "What are you doing?"
She snaps: "You can see perfectly well what I am doing."

I ask: "Why are you writing down my registration number?"
From under the visor of her black baseball cap
She barks: "You have no right
To park your car in the space reserved for
GOLDEN ISLAND EXPECTANT MOTHERS"

I rumble in an avalanche of offended dignity:
"How dare you!
I *am* a Golden Island Expectant Mother!
I am a fifty-eight-years old male of the species
And I have been expecting for nineteen years.
Only last week I had a scan.
Despite you and your terrier
Ireland remains my native land –
My Golden Island –
And I will park where I can.
So go soap your jowls in the jacuzzis of Malaga:
I AM A GOLDEN ISLAND EXPECTANT MOTHER!"

2

The Man with a Bit of Jizz in Him

My husband is a man —
With a bit of jizz in him.
On Monday night in Sligo I said to him:
"Let's go someplace for a week
Before the winter is on top of us."
He said: "Where would you like to go?"
I said: "Down south — West Cork or Kerry."
He said: "Too much hassle."
I said: "Where would you like to go?"
He said: "Dublin Airport early tomorrow morning.
I'll drive halfway, you drive halfway."
We caught the Aer Lingus Dublin–Nice direct flight:
180 Euro return.
Driving to Dublin he phoned his niece in Hertz.
He said: "I want a car in Nice."
Hertz gave us a brand-new Peugeot.
Only thirty miles on the clock.
(If you're over forty-five, they give you a big car.
If you're a young fellow, they give you a small car
That you can go and crash.)
There's only two ways out of Nice Airport —
West or East: simple.
At the first filling station he stopped

And asked the way to St-Paul-de-Vence.
"St-Paul-de-Vence? Exit 48
And do not come on to the motorway again
Until you want to go back to Ireland."
An hour later I was lying on a duvet
In a three-star hotel in St-Paul-de-Vence.
It was spotless. Spotless!
I was that pleased with him I shook his hand
And pulled him in under the duvet with me.
An attractive middle-aged housewife I may be *but* –
There is nothing to beat a man with a bit of jizz in him.

The Wilds of Discretion

His father Matt was a lovely man.
After Susan's husband died
Matt and Susan became great friends.
They went everywhere together.
It was said – I mean, it was thought –
Well, I mean, it was said –
I mean, kindly said –
Well, you know what I mean.
I mean, well, they were close.
They walked the strand together;
They played cards together;
They played golf together;
They did the crossword together.
When they went on holidays together
Well, it was said, naturally,
But I don't mean –

When Matt died, Susan took it badly.
Worse than when her husband died.
Much worse.
They say, they all say,
That it was Matt's death

That – well, you know –
Gave her – well, you know – might
Have given her the –
What killed her.

The day that Matt died
He'd done the crossword with Susan
Back in Susan's cottage.
On his way home he stopped
In the pub for a drink.
Halfway down his glass
He dropped dead.
It was said, I mean it was thought . . .
They were such great friends.

A Robin in Autumn
Chatting at Dawn

Late in the afternoon at the top of the lane
On my way back from a hop to the cliff
I came upon a human – a male – at the gable
Across the lane from the bridge over the mountain stream.
He was middle-aged, overweight, weary, anxious.
Quite like myself.

I uttered nothing and kept *my* head down,
He uttered nothing and kept *his* head down.
Rain clouds split open like rice-bags.
He stared at me as if I could shelter him,
As if I *should* shelter him. He dashed himself
Against the whitewashed, dry-stone wall under the sycamore
And stared at me as if the doomsday had arrived.
If I could have, I would have put a wing around him;
A forlorn, middle-aged man in his Day-Glo green anorak.

While he lurked there in the midnight of the tree
I poked about in the ruts of the lane
Amusing myself, which I do when I can.
The harder the rain teemed, the more revived I felt.
I turned up autumn leaves, gutting their undersides
Of their last midges.

The only real dampener was the human
Feeling sorry for himself and glancing at me
As much as to say: "Poor robin!"
Why are humans so patronising of robins?
They don't mean to be, of course, but they are.
When the storm showed not a sign of abating
He began to slink back up the hill to the cottage.
I stood erect watching his plump rump,
His downcast neck. After he'd departed
I swooped into the nearest fuchsia, preened,
Had a quick perch, a good chirp.

Middle age for any creature is a problematic plummet
But why do humans have to be so crestfallen about it?
With my hands behind my back and my best breast out,
My telescope folded up in my wings, my tricorn gleaming,
I emerge on the bridge of my fuchsia, whistling:
All hands on deck! Hy Brasil, ho!

Achill Island Man

On Achill Island when I wake in the morning
I find myself in the Amusements Arcade of my own body
And I am standing up against the pinball machine
And I insert 20 cents and I give it a kick
And I watch all the small pink balls of pain
Tripping on lights all over my body.
Oh! No!
Toes! Knees! Elbows! Shoulder-blades!
Everywhere I look, small pink balls of pain
And I mind not to rub my neck. Anyways,
I come out of the arcade and I blink
And, despite all the weather
In my body every place I look,
I do have to smile at all those lights
Going on and off. It's amazing, I think,
It's amazing I'm still alive. Oh, man!
No, I never watch television!
I might have colon cancer. I might not.
I might have lumbago or sciatica.
I might have gallstones. I might have ulcers.
I might have diverticulitis!
I might have auricular fibrillation!
I might have diabetes!
As a matter of fact, I do have diabetes,
But with the pills it's all the one.

Will I bother having a haircut?
I will bother having a haircut
And I will get a lift home
In time for the five o'clock removal of my neighbour
Who was seventy-one – she had a year on me –
And who was a very quiet woman, but as good a woman
                as you'd find in all of Achill Island
And after that I will have three pints in The Crossroads Inn –
Maybe four –
And after that I will go home and have my dinner
And after dinner I will go to bed and begin
The whole story all over again – isn't that it?

The Far Side of the Island

Driving over the mountain to the far side of the island
I am brooding neither on what lies ahead of me
Nor on what lies behind me. Up here
On top of the mountain, in the palm of its plateau,
I am being contained by its wrist and its fingertips.

The middle of the journey is what is at stake –
Those twenty-five miles or so of in-betweenness
In which marrow of mortality hardens
In the bones of the nomad. From finite end
To finite end, the orthopaedics of mortality.

Up here on the plateau above the clouds,
Peering down on the clouds in the valleys,
There are no fences, only moorlands
With wildflowers as far as the eye can see;
The earth's unconscious in its own pathology.

Yet when I arrive at the far side of the island
And peer down at the outport on the rocks below,
The Atlantic Ocean rearing raw white knuckles,
Although I am globally sad I am locally glad
To be about to drive down that corkscrew road.

Climbing down the tree-line, past the first cottage,
Past the second cottage, behind every door
A neighbour. It is the company of his kind
Man was born for. Could I have known,
Had I not chanced the far side of the island?

Leave the Curtains Open

I like people looking in at me.
I am proud of my privacy.

Ireland 2001

Where's my bikini?
We'll be late for Mass.

Ireland 2002

Do you ever take a holiday abroad?
No, we always go to America.

Vi

At 93, she is a young girl laughing
At midnight in her doorway.
She cries: "Come again, come again!"
Exhausted, I limp away.

Sandymount Strand Dog Songs

I

Under perishing blue skies
With my bucket and pitchfork,
Digging for worms for bait,
I am a solitary fisherman.
It's a policy of mine
Not to complain
When respectable people
Walking their dogs –
Spaniels, setters,
Labradors, boxers –
From a distance of fifteen yards
Peer down their noses at me
While their loved ones urinate
Into my bucket.
When I get home tonight,
Put my worms in their tray
Of coral sand in my fridge
I'll be on a high.
There's nothing to beat
Your white wrinkler,
All gleaming.
The cod go mad
For your white wrinkler.
Can you imagine?

A stark-raving mad
Besotted cod
Chasing your white wrinkler.
Look at her sensors!
The soft, long, luscious sensors
Of your white wrinkler!
A caterpillar wouldn't be
In the beauty contest,
The Worm of Tralee wouldn't
Be at the dance,
With your white wrinkler.

II

My name is Flaps.
I am a basset hound.
I wouldn't dream
Of urinating into a fisherman's bucket,
Least of all into Bradshaw's
Bucket of glittering wrinklers.
I do not lift my hind leg,
I incline it with a minimum of effort,
The maximum of dignity.
I trot close inshore
Between the shallows twinkling
In the fog and the human species
Power-walking on the promenade.
My ears!
I am vain about the ears –
Vast, velour stage curtains

Sweeping the floor are my
Ears, for which my master
Named me "Flaps".
Normal lifespan
Of a basset hound
Is nine years.
I am twelve and a half years.
But I am feeling great.
Full of dog I am today,
Full of hound,
Basset to the universe,
Low to the sand,
Flush to the planet.
True, I've a dicky heart,
But I'm on medication
And on a day like today –
Under perishing blue skies –
Dublin Bay sprayed in fog –
I could pad forever.
I love everything
About Sandymount Strand
But let's be plain-spoken.
What I love most
Are the females –
O the basset females.
I'm a hundred and twenty
Human years old,
But I feel the same about
Basset females
As I did when Mary Robinson

Pitched her kennels
In the Phoenix Park.
Here's a basset female now,
The spitting image of Mary Robinson.
In spite of my age
I'll flap my ears at her.
With luck she'll squeal.
It's the combination
Of my black-and-tan coat
With my toothpaste-white
Trotters and my great age
That dazzles them.

III

My name is Teeny –
Teeny Myles – and I
Am seventy-nine and I
Live at 175
Sandymount Strand, next
Door to Fifi who is
Ninety-four and
Make no mistake about it,
It is a perishing day
In Dublin Bay.
At seventy-nine I'm a nipper
Compared with Fifi Geldof
Next door at ninety-four,
Beetling around in her Volks.
It's a perishing day,

But I am rejoicing in it,
Walking my dog Cara
On Sandymount Strand,
Talking to other dogs.
I know people
By their dogs.
He may look like a dingo,
But he's a mixture of all
The dogs that ever were.
Got him from a rescue home.
You, sir, have no dog,
Why have you no dog?
A pity. I'm sorry.
Depressed by the
War in Iraq, are you?
Stupid war.
My father fought in two wars.
I – I
Am never depressed and
I have lived all my life
At 175 Sandymount Strand.
It's a house, you know,
That's 180 years old and
The foundations are – are –
I have *great* foundations.
I have *deep* foundations.
Never a sniff of damp.
I go to church in
St Peter's in Donnybrook.
Oh no, I never go to St John's.

Too high, too high.
So you're a poet, sir?
There's a poet near us.
One night I called to his door
Collecting for the British Legion.
He declined. So funny.
He writes poetry,
But it doesn't rhyme.
Does your poetry rhyme?
Oh I don't like
Poetry that doesn't rhyme.
No, I'll walk, but
Thank you so much
For your offer of a lift.
I don't mind the rain.
I never have minded rain
And I never wear a hat
And my hair is my own.
One day on my bike I
Knocked down another lady
In O'Connell Street –
O'Connell Street! –
And her wig fell off.
War is not depressing,
It's stupid.
Cheerio! And thank you!

HEADLINES

At 8.40 a.m. on the morning of Sunday, 7 September 2003 on an island in Upper Lough Erne, County Fermanagh, Northern Ireland, an elderly couple, Mr and Mrs John James Reihill, stepped out of their farmhouse where the Reihill family have lived and farmed for generations and walked down the path through the fir trees and the hydrangeas to the shore in whose reeds their small rowing boat nestled, stepped in and set off across the waters of the lough to attend 9 a.m. Mass on the mainland in the Holy Cross Church in Lisnaskea. In Jerusalem the Israeli Prime Minister Ariel Sharon threatened to assassinate the Palestinian leader Yasser Arafat who the day before had compelled his own Prime Minister, Mahmoud Abbas, to resign. In Baghdad the US Defense Secretary Mr Donald Rumsfeld, who was due to address US troops in Tikrit, had to cancel his address for fear of being heckled by his troops. In Belfast, Mr Gerry Adams reiterated his "firm view" that in the light of the discovery of the remains of Mrs Jean McConville in Shilling Beach and next week's excavation of a Monaghan bog for the remains of Mr Columba McVeigh, and in order that these excavations may bring "closure" to grieving families, it would be better for all concerned not to speak in public any further about the missing bodies of innocent people murdered thirty years ago by the IRA. In Dublin on radio, television and in the newspapers, serious discussions were held on the merits of rival TV chat shows. Mrs Reihill sat in the bow of the rowing boat in her brown Sunday dress, low black-heeled shoes, long green overcoat and white leather handbag with gold chain. Mr Reihill sat in the corner of the stern and switched on the ignition of the outboard engine. The small craft lifted its bow in the air and, as Mr Reihill sat low in the water, Mrs Reihill gazed down at her husband in his black corduroy cap, his black bespoke suit, his black-laced size eleven shoes and his ankle-length black-belted leather greatcoat. He seemed to smile through his bespectacled beard, but neither of them spoke. A sentinel heron watched from a stone and five swans sailed in procession past them. At Mass in Lisnaskea they heard the priest read from the Gospel of St Mark, 7: 31-37, where Jesus makes a deaf-and-dumb man hear and speak. Jesus said to the man: "Ephphatha," that is, "Be opened." After Mass and after chatting for three quarters of an hour with Mass-goers, Mr and Mrs John James Reihill visited the newsagents where, tomorrow being their wedding anniversary, each, without the other knowing, purchased a wedding anniversary card before making the return journey across the waters of the lough to their island home. Their sheepdog Bonny lay smiling on the wooden jetty. Pacing up behind his wife through the fir trees and the hydrangeas with his hands clasped behind his back Mr Reihill announced slowly and magniloquently to Mrs Reihill: "John James Reihill needs a cup of tea before he goes any further."

The Celtic Tiger

I am an unmarried mother –
Tomorrow is my twenty-second birthday –
And I am waiting for the Number 3 bus
From the power station
To bring my five-year-old son Jack to the clinic.
I was reared in the orphanage.
I loved it in the orphanage.
The nuns were cool,
Especially Sister Louise.
She was my best friend.
She was awesome.
But one day when I was sixteen
I was told to go downstairs
To the parlour beside the hall door.
There was a man and a woman.
They smiled: "We are your parents
And we've come to take you home."
I cried tears and I begged
Sister Louise to keep me
And Sister Louise cried tears,
But I was taken away.
That same day my parents
Sold me to a man called Kirwan –
They didn't tell me his Christian name –

Kirwan is all they kept calling him –
Kirwan! Kirwan!
That night Kirwan raped me.
He was like a looney. His mickey
Had bits of potato on it.
He kept it up all night.
Roaring, moaning, beating me.
Nine months later I had my lovely little boy, Jack.

II

I am my parents' youngest daughter
And they are so proud of me
For all kinds of reasons,
But principally because I earn
300, 000 Euro a year
As a corporate solicitor in Dublin
And I am only thirty-one.
They are so proud of my lifestyle.
I own three houses and I buy
Two or three new outfits a week
And I holiday in the Seychelles
And I am always in a relationship.
I am never not in a relationship.
My parents really are so proud of me.
Children? No way!

The Annual Mass of the Knights of Columbanus

Although I am a bishop I think
I deserve, almost as much as the next man,
A degree of compassion and understanding.
There is nothing I would not do –
Or at least not *try* to do –
In the fulfilment of my obligations,
But I hesitate at having to say Mass
For the Knights of Columbanus.
I not only hesitate, I balk.
In fact, I sweat. I shiver.

To call a crosier a crosier
Or – where I come from – a wheelbarrow a wheelbarrow,
I cannot abide the Knights of Columbanus.
All those feathers and plumes and medallions
And starched wing collars and velveteen tailcoats
And chains and tricorn hats.
What a collection of high-faluting layabouts.
In this day and age of democracy and terror
There is no place in my mundane opinion
For such orgies of sanctimonious militarism;
Such pantomimes of piotiousness.

Yet here I am on the orders of the Cardinal
At half-past eleven on a Saturday morning
In the sacristy of the Cathedral in Galway
Preparing to celebrate the Holy Mass
For these effigies of pomposity,
These lechers of superfluous affluence.

Lord, help me to get through your Mass
Without having too many bad thoughts,
Especially at the Eucharist.
How I dread having to dispense Communion
To these whited sepulchres
Who insist on taking Communion on the tongue
Instead of in the hand.
Isn't it, O Lord, but yet another exhibition
Of ill-concealed conceit –
Taking Communion on the tongue?
They like sticking their tongues out
And putting their phlegmy, stalactite throats on parade
With their hands on their ceremonial swords,
Up to their hilts in wilful vanity,
Legal gobbledegook, real estate, indifference.

Dear God, when I have finished vesting and robing,
Please change me into a horse of a bishop
So that on the altar I can whinny
From time to time to let off steam.
Now – now am I ready?
To trot out onto the altar
And before beginning Mass

Give the Knights and their consorts
A neigh to remember.
That's it, a neigh to remember!

Canon James O. Hannay Pays a Return Visit to the Old Rectory, Westport, County Mayo, 8 October 2000

The lines are fallen unto me in pleasant places;
yea, I have a goodly heritage.

The Old Rectory has long since passed out of the hands of
the Church of Ireland.

In 1982 it was purchased by young Seamus Walsh, one of the
Walshes of Bridge Street.

His father Willie Walsh who had the pub was married to
that wondrous Hughes woman Delia.

(Her uncle Charles Hughes – a most pleasant man and a
most pleasing man –

Was the first Chairman of Westport Urban District Council.)

Young Seamus and his wife Mary MacBride, the fair lady
also from Bridge Street,

Grand-niece of the Major – the audacious, wandering Major –

(Her grandfather Hugh Coen opened his drapery shop in
the course of *my* lifetime)

Have reared their family, one son and four daughters, in the
Old Rectory.

Seamus is a roofer. Self-employed, he has his own business

In Carna in Connemara. Why Carna?

Because he likes to speak Irish when and where he can,
At home or at work, without having to make a fuss,
Just as he likes to play the piano impromptu, informally –
Victorian ballads or Moore's *Melodies* or Gilbert and Sullivan
Or hits from *Cats* or *Evita.*
He has five men working for him full-time, five part-time.
No man has worked harder for his wife and children
Than the same Seamus Walsh. His wife and children want for nothing.
The cynics of the town – of whom there are the same quota
As in my time – the town lawyers, the town know-alls –
Knowingly wink and nod when the chat is about Seamus:
"The New Ireland" they dub him and they guffaw
At the idea of the Old Rectory being amok with the Barbie dolls,
Pop-star posters, Play Stations, Nike trainers of the Walsh family
And the phenomenon of the head of the house
Being a Roman Catholic roofer and not a Church of Ireland clergyman.
When he is not putting a new roof on a house in Clifden
Or driving one of his children to music and drama
Or football or swimming or running and jumping
Or taking out his wife to dinner in "La Bella Vista"
Seamus Walsh may be found browsing his bedside books –
John Moriarty, The Messenger, Ulysses.
He exudes the physicality of the wild, pilgrim spirit,
The spirituality of fierce, hard work
And I, Canon James O. Hannay (alias George A. Birmingham),
Who was lazy, but by no means the idlest of men,
Back in my old home, the Old Rectory in Westport –
Of the psalmist's pleasant places, pleasantest of many –
Have to say that I am mindful with envy
At its twenty-first-century atmosphere of carefree sanctity.

The Carnalurgan Milkman

I am the black sheep of the family.
On bright, warm, summer evenings
In front of the whole family –
All those solicitors, all those barristers –
My mother smiles at me and pipes up:
"Why don't you go and live in Australia?"
And I smile also and we all smile,
Because we know that mother means what she says.

I play the chimes on the tits
Astride my three-legged stool;
Least of all the faithful, utterly despised by many,
I am the Carnalurgan Milkman.

Every covie knows what I live for:
For my small, hilly fields in Carnalurgan
In the foothills of the Himalaya
(Westport people call Croagh Patrick "the Himalaya"!).
When the family deign to visit me in my fields
They remain seated in their cars.
How many hours in wet rain have I stood cross-legged
At the windows of the cars of the lawyers of Ireland?

I play the chimes on the tits
Astride my three-legged stool;

Least of all the faithful, utterly despised by many,
I am the Carnalurgan Milkman.

I am keen on my cows, although I confess it myself.
I am keen to get up early on black winter mornings
And drive out in the dark to my fields
To milk my own cows, to bottle my own milk,
And ride around the empty, still sleeping town,
Setting down bottles on windowsills, in doorways;
And I think of all those latchicos and lebidjehs
Still snoring in their scratchers, scratching themselves.

I play the chimes on the tits
Astride my three-legged stool;
Least of all the faithful, utterly despised by many,
I am the Carnalurgan Milkman.

I lean on my pitchfork at noon in the sun
On top of my drumlin overlooking Clew Bay,
Watching herds of white horses swarming in
On the wind from the west, listening
To the seaweed on the rocks crackling
As it awakes to the heat, inhaling
The salt and the iodine. I may
Have arthritis, but I am a free man.

I play the chimes on the tits
Astride my three-legged stool;
Least of all the faithful, utterly despised by many,
I am the Carnalurgan Milkman.

33

Thanks be to God I got married
To a working woman – a haberdasher
In Bridge Street, a draper,
A vendor of hosiery and lingerie.
That's a word that can trip a man up –
Lingerie! When a covie tries to rise me
With a "Your better half sells what?"
I enlighten him slowly: "Lingerie."

I play the chimes on the tits
Astride my three-legged stool;
Least of all the faithful, utterly despised by many,
I am the Carnalurgan Milkman.

But I am also the Bridge Street Haberdasher
On Saturday afternoons when udderless
I help out the missus in the shop.
My daughter boasts – and who am I
To deny my fair-haired Mary? –
There is no man in Westport to beat me
In the lost art of sealing wax
And the tying up of a parcel with twine.

I play the chimes on the tits
Astride my three-legged stool;
Least of all the faithful, utterly despised by many,
I am the Carnalurgan Milkman.

But Jesus Christ! The first question
You always ask me, dearest great granddaughter,

Even this afternoon on my deathbed,
Is what age am I?
Like my father's father's fathers before me
I am no age. And you,
My daughter's daughter's daughter,
You are ageless, PLEASE listen to me.

I play the chimes on the tits
Astride my three-legged stool;
Least of all the faithful, utterly despised by many
I am the Carnalugan Milkman.

The New Presbytery, Westport, County Mayo

My father was the first married parish priest of Westport.
We lived in the New Presbytery on the Mall
Under the slope of the Fair Green –
A stone's throw from Toby's Bar –
Where the Carrowbeg River makes a right turn
West into the Mall, on down to the Demesne.
Our front door was south-facing on to the Mall
And our east gable was part of the river wall.
The river in spate raced under our kitchen window
Where our mother spent most of her life
Cooking the most scrumptious suppers.
She was all home-maker, Mother was.

I loved my father and although he was a priest
He only sometimes overdid it, keen
To answer every question with a biblical quotation.
He was no goody-goody, my reverend father.
No man relished a good pint more than he.
No man enjoyed a good game of golf
On our championship course at Carraholly
More than he, and he never agonised about it.
If he missed a putt or if he socketed

Or if he had a fresh air
He didn't bury himself under duvets of melancholia.

But there was one thing my father was holier about
Than any other priest I have known –
Except for Archbishop Cassidy of Tuam –
And that was his dedication to homily-composition.
When he was dying – of natural causes –
It came as no surprise to me
When he confessed that at his ordination
In Maynooth in the Dark Ages
He made a private promise, a secret vow,
That no matter what, he would always
Give his all to his Sunday sermon.

I think my father spent much of every week of his life
Sketching and jotting down notes for his Sunday sermon.
So it was never less than pure poetry, pure passion.
Always making pure sense.
Wind, rain, fog, hailstones or sunlight,
By Friday night when he sat down
In his cubby-hole in the cellar
To type up and print out his sermon
He had the guts of a spiritual scoop.

From far and near people came to 10.30 a.m. Mass
In St Mary's Church in Westport,
Simply to hear Dad's sermon, which was

Never less than inspiringly cool.
I used close my eyes
And, listening to the mountain of his soul,
Watch the bog cotton of his thoughts
Sprinkle the moors of his prose.

The New Presbytery was not only the parish priest's
    house;
It was our home, our Elysium, our Westport cove,
Our pile of treasure trove.
There were five of us children and for all of us
The leaving of the New Presbytery was always a trauma,
Even when it was to go on holiday to Barcelona
Or on an Erasmus to Salamanca.
How could it have been otherwise?
The badgers at the back of the garden!
Mink, also, stinking like skunk!
The clothes line rigged from sycamore to sycamore
Flying all our delicates, all our primary colours.
The castor-oil tree grinning like a clown!
The granite flags of the patio!
All the hydrangeas of the spectrum –
Blue hydrangea, pink hydrangea, white hydrangea.
"What hydrangeas need is iron!"
That was Mother's war-cry.
She used collect any old iron
And bury all of it under hydrangea.
The front steps of old red sandstone!
The cast-iron boot-scraper! The brass knocker!
Urns, window-boxes, watering cans!

Petunias peering out the windows like chipper spinsters!
Polished chestnuts gleaming in blue gravel!
Pampas grasses high in their own Ethiopias
Shaking their spears at Croagh Patrick!
The sleepers from the disused railway line to the Quay,
Which formed both a path and a pergola!
The two red, rusted, iron, famine soup cauldrons!
The white-washed wall of pink clematis!
The ceanothus at the door – Mother's favourite!
The bright green lime, the girth of which
Signified a tree older than the house itself,
The New Presbytery,
Erected over two hundred years ago.
What used Dad say?
"Tonight you will be with me in heaven!"

Asylum Seeker

Hurtling along the road from Castlebar to Westport
In my filthy, two-door, bottle-green Opel Astra,
The last stage of the drive from Dublin,
Five miles out from Westport I catch my first glimpse of
          Croagh Patrick,
The mountain of my birth,
Being stark gently,
Bluely-greyly.

Croagh Patrick, the Reek –
Ararat of Armenia –
Let no Turk try to still my feet –
O Westport in the Light of Asia Minor –
The mountain whose long hands are steepled in prayer,
Whose ten fingers are twinned at their tips
Posing the question
To which no man of salt knows the answer.

My head drops onto the driving wheel,
My accelerator sobs,
For I am almost home. Here
Only is where I can call "home"
Under the Westport skyline
Where I know I can seek asylum;
Where seven thousand years ago

When sea wrestled sky
Noah also did seek asylum.

Here is where I can drop
Dead in the sub-zero dawn outside
Any man's front door and not
Be rolled over and kicked into the gutter.
Here is where the young curate will bless
My old man's baby corpse
And a pass-the-hat-round will get me
A cubby-hole in the clay in Aughawall cemetery
Under the MacBride cairn
Under the holy mountain of my birth –
Croagh Patrick on the Westport skyline.

Tonight at twilight
I land into Westport from Dublin,
Into a huddle of snowdrops under a scarf of crows
In the schoolyard of the bare treetops
At playtime, bedtime,
Cawing, cackling, chasing, circling,
And one yellow crocus under an aged lime,
And green schools of daffodils
About to wake up into their fate of gold
Three days before Ash Wednesday.
I fling up into the darkening sky
The pancakes of my soul
And jump into the arms of my fleeting god-daughter
As she steps up into a white minibus to transport her to her
    bower.

The Westport Ethiopian

Last Saturday the 28th of February 2004
At the Connacht Junior & Senior Indoor Championships
In the indoor tartan and banked track in Nenagh, Co
   Tipperary
In the Girls' Under 13s' 600 metres
I saw an eleven-year-old Ethiopian girl
Running in the green-and-red top
Of the Westport Athletic Club:
Maria Caterina Walassie.
Only it seemed to me that she was not really running,
She was making music with her gazelle legs
And the track was the stave, all crotchets and semi-quavers,
Along which, sight-reading, she was striding out
In grace-notes of lopes and bounds.
She won by about fifty-five metres,
But it did not look like winning
So much as chanting
In the old, slow, formal, Ethiopian way.
It was a kind of long-legged chanting –
Chanting the chorus of an ancient tribal chant
Of the lands of her forefathers:
"Over the mountains and far away
In the city of the wise king."

The 2003 World Snooker Championship

Don't lecture me about lint on the baize –
I am ninety-six years of age.

What an old woman like me needs
More than a meal or medicine
Or a life sentence in a nursing home
Is seventeen days in front of the television
In my own home
Watching the World Snooker Championship
In the Crucible in Sheffield.
Although I like rugby,
I am a snooker fanatic.

Don't lecture me about lint on the baize –
I am ninety-six years of age.

I am frail and cranky
And I have a pain in my neck
That would make Humpty Dumpty
Grateful to fall off his wall,
But at a crucial moment in the Crucible
I sizzle with satisfaction
At the spectacle of a young man's bottom

43

As he bends down low over the green baize
To pot the black –
A superbly turned-out young man's trim bottom,
The left cheek of which is streamlined
With shoe heel and collar bone
When he lifts his left leg to spread-eagle it
Like a pedigree cocker spaniel
Along the kerb of the table.

Don't lecture me about lint on the baize –
I am ninety-six years of age.

And when that young man hails
From Ranelagh, Dublin 6,
And when his name is Ken
I am as much a believer in the Resurrection
As the Pope in Rome.
If there is a heaven –
One must not say so
But I doubt it –
Heaven would be the Triangle at night
Of snooker tables lit by floodlights
Under the whites of whose eyes
Thousands upon thousands upon thousands
Of trim-bottomed young men
Would be chalking their cues
Before focussing their perfect pelvises
On the white cue ball,

The red and the black,
And on all the coloured balls –
All the coloured balls.

Don't lecture me about lint on the baize –
I am ninety-six years of age.

The Beautiful Game

Sunday afternoon in August, sunny, warm,
Watching TV – the beautiful game
Being played with professional ugliness,
Manchester United versus Aston Villa.
My floor littered with the customary Sabbath garbage:
Newspapers, newspapers, more newspapers.

Such a tender knock on the door, I wonder –
Did I imagine it?
I unlock it and see before me
A handsome, middle-aged woman
In dull gold tank-top, dull gold slacks.
I have never seen her before in my life.

I peer out at her over my reading specs,
Not knowing what to say to her,
Saying "Yes?"
She does not speak, but returns
My perplexed, anxious gaze.
She says: "Nessa."

"Oh Nessa!"
We'd been married for fifteen years
A long time ago.
I switch off the TV,

Interrupting
The beautiful game.

"I am on my way back to Cork."
Twenty minutes later she resumes her journey,
Driving away in her blue machine.
I do not switch back on the TV.
I have had more than enough,
For one afternoon, of the beautiful game.

Sleeping Nude

after Sarah Longley

If you could see me as I am,
Nude in my sleeping in my rented room
You might have mercy on my body,
My uprooted, rootless body
Leaf-heaped, leaf-reeking on my bed
On my right side and clinging
To a pillow or hugging it or supine
With one knee raised or face down
Amid my hips, a frog beseeching,
And conclude that every human animal
No matter how bold or timid, bestial or angelic,
When topped to the forehead with naked sleep
Is a suckling at its mother's breast,
Born to breathe, fated to rest.

"Women are Brutally Practical People"

Antoinette says she never sees smoke coming from
your chimney, Paul.
Is there anything the matter, Paul?

The Wisdom of Ex-Wives

When on the phone to my ex-wife
I admitted I was lonely,
She said: "Why don't you play golf
If you're feeling lonely?"

I said: "Who would I play with?"
She said: "Can't you play on your own?"
That's the sort of thing ex-wives say:
"Can't you play on your own?"

I hooted down the phone:
"Playing on your own is an *oxymoron!*"
I wanted to change the subject and to say goodbye,
And to stand up and cry.

Dancing with Leo

Leo is the strong, silent type,
Tall, erect, moustached, round-shouldered,
Humble as an ox,
Proud as a cock.
So the way we get to do our own thing
Is to dance with our cars.

I live downstairs.
Leo lives upstairs.
We never speak.
(In two-and-a-half years
We have never spoken –
Not even when we're speaking to each other.)
But when the coast is clear
And there is no one else in the house
I sit into my car and I drive it
From one side of the gravel
To the other – a bottle-green Opel Astra.
Five minutes later, fifteen at most,
Leo comes downstairs and ambles out the door
And across the iron bars of my basement window –
O my heart, O his feet –
And he slides into his driving seat
And he drives his car – a silver Mazda –
From one side of the gravel to the other.

We always make certain never to park our cars
On the same side of the gravel.
Snowdrops and daffodils, O you're breaking my heart!
That is our dance.
Nothing in our Tax-Designated Area
Is so satisfying, so cool,
As dancing with Leo.

Admission

Driving myself to hospital – the Regional –
I have to believe what I am seeing:
A funeral in front of me.

Is it permitted to overtake a funeral?
On this road of so many bends?
Of "accident black spots"?

I'm late for my hospital check-in,
But they'd hardly not keep my bed?
They'd hardly give away my bed?

After two miles we hit a straight.
Three hundred yards and nothing coming.
I accelerate, chopping down into third.

Doing fifty I start to pass out the hearse
Only to confront an approaching car.
I flash my lights, but to no avail.

She – it is a *she* – she forces me
To swerve in behind the hearse –
Between the hearse and the mourners' limousine.

I can see their faces in my rear-view mirror.
How stricken their faces appear!
So am I – stricken!

Why on earth did she have to do that to me?
Head-girl smirk, lacquered hair.
Where is my life going?

I stare at the coffin in front of my nose.
Pricey oak – and why not?
The driver in uniform puffing his pipe.

At the hospital reception I am told
That my bed has been taken.
For seven hours I sit in a corridor

Praying for support to the late Donal McCann.
Adamantly he insists: "Flow with the stream."
That I do, and I find myself

No longer livid with fear
But thinking of Mrs Ferrari –
The fish-and-chip lady

At her window opposite the main door
Of St Patrick's Church
In her Day-Glo pink shop coat

And of the way she always inquires
"Salt and vinegar?"
With the faintest of faintest smiles

Like a surgeon after an operation.
To the red man sitting opposite me
Under the flaky, distempered wall

I stammer: "No vinegar – salt please."
He snaps: "Are *you* talking to *me*?"
I admit it: "I am."

In a bed at last, in a bedlam ward,
Under a TV on a black gantry,
I think of my car all alone in the car park.

A 97 Opel Astra. Maroon. MH 1504.
People are so nosey: "Why the Meath reg?"
It's where *she* lives. The woman that was.

Rosie Joyce

I

That was that Sunday afternoon in May
When a hot sun pushed through the clouds
And you were born!

I was driving the two hundred miles from west to east,
The sky blue-and-white china in the fields
In impromptu picnics of tartan rugs;

When neither words nor I
Could have known that you had been named already
And that your name was Rosie –

Rosie Joyce! May you some day in May
Fifty-six years from today be as lucky
As I was when you were born that Sunday:

To drive such side-roads, such main roads, such ramps, such
    roundabouts,
To cross such bridges, to by-pass such villages, such towns
As I did on your Incarnation Day.

By-passing Swinford – Croagh Patrick in my rear-view mirror –
My cell phone rang and, stopping on the hard edge of

    P. Flynn's highway,
I heard Mark your father say:

"A baby girl was born at 3.33 p.m.
Weighing 7 and a 1/2 lbs in Holles Street.
Tough work, all well."

II

That Sunday in May before daybreak
Night had pushed up through the slopes of Achill
Yellow forefingers of Arum Lily – the first of the year;

Down at the Sound the first rhododendrons
Purpling the golden camps of whins;
The first hawthorns powdering white the mainland;

The first yellow irises flagging roadside streams;
Quills of bog-cotton skimming the bogs;
Burrishoole cemetery shin-deep in forget-me-nots;

The first sea pinks speckling the seashore;
Cliffs of London Pride, groves of bluebell,
First fuchsia, Queen Anne's Lace, primrose.

I drove the Old Turlough Road, past Walter Durcan's Farm,
Umbrella'd in the joined handwriting of its ash trees;
I drove Tulsk, Kilmainham, the Grand Canal.

Never before had I felt so fortunate

To be driving back into Dublin city;
Each canal bridge an old pewter brooch.

I rode the waters and the roads of Ireland,
Rosie, to be with you, seashell at my ear!
How I laughed when I cradled you in my hand.

Only at Tarmonbarry did I slow down,
As in my father's Ford Anglia half a century ago
He slowed down also, as across the River Shannon

We crashed, rattled and bounced on a Bailey bridge;
Daddy relishing his role as Moses,
Enunciating the name of the Great Divide

Between the East and the West!
We are the people of the West,
Our fate to go East.

No such thing, Rosie, as a Uniform Ireland
And please God there never will be;
There is only the River Shannon and all her sister rivers

And all her brother mountains and their family prospects.
There are higher powers than politics
And these we call wildflowers or, geologically, people.

Rosie Joyce – that Sunday in May
Not alone did you make my day, my week, my year
To the prescription of Jonathan Philbin Bowman –

Daymaker!
Daymaker!
Daymaker!

Popping out of my daughter, your mother –
Changing the expressions on the faces all around you –
All of them looking like blue hills in a heat haze –

But you saved my life. For three years
I had been subsisting in the slums of despair,
Unable to distinguish one day from the next.

III

On the return journey from Dublin to Mayo
In Charlestown on Main Street
I meet John Normanly, organic farmer from Curry.

He is driving home to his wife Caroline
From a Mountbellew meeting of the Western Development
    Commission
Of Dillon House in Ballaghadereen.

He crouches in his car, I waver in the street,
As we exchange lullabies of expectancy;
We wet our foreheads in John Moriarty's autobiography.

The following Sunday is the Feast of the Ascension
Of Our Lord into Heaven:
Thank You, O Lord, for the Descent of Rosie onto Earth.

The Proud Cry of the
Young Father

Standing in the middle of the kitchen of his new home,
Which he built with his own hands,
The young father throws his seven-month-old baby daughter
   high up into the air
Almost grazing the ceiling –
Beatrice (Bee for short) –
And her young mother, the bee-keeper, at the table smiles:
"Be sure and catch her on the way down."

"Oh I will!" he cries.
"Oh I'll be sure to catch her on the way down!"
He cries proudly from the Ontario of his soul;
He whose young man's voice was a Buffalo whisper
Has become all of Ontario, all wilderness and garden,
All hard work and all play;
A polar cry hopping up and down the cosmos.

The 12 O'Clock Mass,
Roundstone, County Galway,
28 July 2002

On Sunday the 28th of July 2002 –
The summer it rained almost every day –
In rain we strolled down the road
To the church on the hill overlooking the sea.
I had been told to expect "a fast Mass".
Twenty minutes. A piece of information
Which disconcerted me.

Out onto the altar hurried
A short, plump priest in late middle age
With a horn of silver hair,
In green chasuble billowing
Like a poncho or a caftan over
White surplice and a pair
Of Reeboks – mammoth trainers.

He whizzed along,
Saying the readings himself as well as the Gospel;
Yet he spoke with conviction and with clarity;
His every action an action
Of what looked like effortless concentration;

Like Tiger Woods on top of his form.
His brief homily concluded with a solemn request.

To the congregation he gravely announced:
"I want each of you to pray for a special intention,
A very special intention.
I want each of you – in the sanctity of your own souls –
To pray that, in the All-Ireland
Championship hurling quarter-final this afternoon in Croke
    Park,
Clare will beat Galway."

The congregation splashed into laughter
And the church became a church of effortless prayer.
He whizzed through the Consecration
As if the Consecration was something
That occurs at every moment of the day and night;
As if betrayal and the overcoming of betrayal
Were an every-minute occurrence.

As if the Consecration was the "now"
In the "now" of the Hail Mary prayer:
"Pray for us *now* and at the hour of our death."
At the Sign of Peace he again went sombre
As he instructed the congregation:
"I want each of you to turn around and say to each other:
'You are beautiful.'"

The congregation was flabbergasted, but everyone fluttered

And swung around and uttered that extraordinary phrase:
"You are beautiful."
I shook hands with at least five strangers,
Two men and three women, to each of them saying:
"You are beautiful." And they to me:
"You are beautiful."

At the end of Mass, exactly twenty-one minutes,
The priest advised: "Go now and enjoy yourselves
For that is what God made you to do –
To go out there and enjoy yourselves
And to pray that, in the All-Ireland
Championship hurling quarter-final between Clare and
    Galway
In Croke Park, Clare will win."

After Mass, the rain had drained away
Into a tide of sunlight on which we sailed out
To St Macdara's Island and dipped our sails –
Both of us smiling, radiant sinners.
In a game of pure delight, Clare beat Galway by one point:
Clare 1 goal and 17 points, Galway 19 points.
"Pray for us *now* and at the hour of our death."

Michael Hartnett, the Poet King

The poet went to his hotel room and sitting on the edge of
the bed wished he were dead.

"O God," he said, "I have had enough. Take my life; I am no
better than my ancestors."

Then he lay down and went to sleep.

But his soul stayed awake and said, "Get up and eat."

He rummaged in his carrier bag and found a doughnut and
a bottle of still water.

He ate and drank and then lay down again.

But his soul said to him a second time, "Get up and eat, or
you will not be able to give the poetry reading tonight."

So he got up and ate and drank, and made a cup of tea with
a teabag, and strengthened by that food he went on giving
poetry readings for forty years until he reached the hospi-
tal where he gladly, not sadly, died.

Forty years ago he would have been glad to know that forty
years later he would gladly, not sadly, die.

Beatrice Monti della Corte von Rezzori

I am here in a tower in Tuscany.
It is April and the weather is cold,
Just a little bit sunny. There's a military jet
Ripping up the sky
En route to Afghanistan
Or the Middle East,
And here's the rain again
Feeding the red earth,
Squirting bliss into oak,
Lime, ravines of acacia
Budding in beads of pearl;
Fern, moss, walnut, mulberry,
Capsules of forget-me-not;
Stillness, but for birdsong;
Exclusiveness, elusiveness;
Otherworld, middleworld;
Vineyards, olive groves;
Dovecote, chicken coop;
Stands of orange-coned laurel pine;
Skylines backlit by black cypresses.

Having a bath in the Tower –
Although there is no Mrs Durcan
To scrub my back
And the Jews and the Arabs
Are at it again,
War worse than before,
At prayer and at slaughter –
When they are at prayer
Is best time to slaughter –
And the Christians doing nothing
Except peddling and meddling,
I am praising the name
(For that's all I know of her)
Of the woman who made
This bathroom out of nothing;
Its whitewashed walls
Frescoed with a plant
That flowers to the beak
Of an in-coming bird;
Its green fronds frilled,
Its petals wide-eyed.
She cries: "Thanks God."
Her name is Beatrice.
Delighted to meet you,
Beatrice –
Beatrice Monti
della Corte von Rezzori.

Having a bath in the Tower –
Although there is no Mrs Durcan
To empty my waste-paper basket
And glue back together again
The torn-up drafts of my genius,
And the Pope and his cardinals
Refuse to say sorry
To the children their priests
Have terrorised
And the Queen Mother is dead
At a hundred-and-one, who chirped
"It's 80 per cent disappointment, maybe
More, but it's such fun" –
She was speaking of steeple chasing –
I am praising the name
(For that's all I know of her)
Of the woman who made
This bathroom out of nothing;
Its low, timber roof beams
Of pine and of cedar
Slope to a kneeling-space,
And its day-bed
Upholstered in understated
Chrysanthemums on beige.
Her name is Beatrice.
Delighted to meet you,
Beatrice –
Beatrice Monti
della Corte von Rezzori.

Having a bath in the Tower –
Although there is no Mrs Durcan
To take down dictation,
And refugees from all
Over the world on the
Go like the Goths
And the Visigoths sixteen
Hundred years ago –
In Black Tuscany
Albanian princesses
Working as chambermaids
And Sardinian princes
Working as handymen
And Berber shepherds
Working as chauffeurs
And Nigerians and Somalis
On all the street-corners
Of Florence and Arezzo
Selling black umbrellas –
I am praising the name
(For that's all I know of her)
Of the woman who made
This bathroom out of nothing
With its bidet face to
Face with its lavatory,
Its bidet-butt to the door,
And the three-panel cream screen
With its pastoral sketches,
Its centre-piece a square tower

Beside a squatter round tower
On a cliff with a mountain
Ravine far down below
Whose blue, velvet-like
Rocks receive the remains
Of recycled lovers tossed
Out of Donna Olympia's
Top-storey bedroom loophole.
Her name is Beatrice.
Delighted to meet you,
Beatrice –
Beatrice Monti
della Corte von Rezzori.

Having a bath in the Tower –
Although there is no Mrs Durcan
To entice me to resist
And the Americans
Under Bush itch
To go to war,
Any war, preferably
World war,
Thermonuclear world war
Under bare pink bottoms,
Under Auntie Condoleezza
Rice and Granpa Rumsfeld,
I am praising the name
(For that's all I know of her)
Of the woman who made

This bathroom out of nothing
With its low, long, narrow, white table
And a jigsaw puzzle with
"Over 500 Interlocking Pieces".
(If only I myself
Could discover a piece
With which to interlock –
That is the jigsaw
I am dying to do.)
Her name is Beatrice.
Delighted to meet you,
Beatrice –
Beatrice Monti
della Corte von Rezzori.

Having a bath in the Tower –
Although there is no Mrs Durcan
To run the bath or to pull
The plug or to towel
A man down fortissimo
And in the democracies
Majorities of populations
Do not know how to
Cope with leisure
And young men are so bored
That they carry knives
And electorates are too lazy
Or browbeaten or wasted
Or selfish or baffled
To come out and vote

I am praising the name
(For that's all I know of her)
Of the woman who made
This bathroom out of nothing
With its floral, cream and pink
China chamber pot
Catching the leak
Under the hot radiator.
Her name is Beatrice.
Delighted to meet you,
Beatrice –
Beatrice Monti
della Corte von Rezzori.

Having a bath in the Tower –
Although there is no Mrs Durcan
To turn on the cold tap
And pour cold water
Over ego and ego's willie,
And making my racial will
Is not a priority –
That's a matter for boys
And girls eager for medals
In the Culture Olympics –
And the Irish hire jets
To deport Nigerians
Attenzione!
Berlusconi!
TELEVISION – LUXURY – THE FAMILY
And in Queensland

A backpacking teenage girl
Is robbed and flung over
A bridge to her death,
And Uncle Colin Powell
Is scuttling about in Jerusalem
As sideways as possible,
I am praising the name
(For that's all I know of her)
Of the woman who made
This bathroom out of nothing,
Shelving the bidet and lavatory,
The alcove of six bookshelves,
The bottom two empty
Except for rolls of soft-lit
Richter toilet paper;
2001: A Space Odyssey
By Arthur C. Clarke;
The Manchurian Candidate
By Richard Condon;
The Valley of Fear
By Sir Arthur Conan Doyle;
Her name is Beatrice.
Delighted to meet you,
Beatrice –
Beatrice Monti
della Corte von Rezzori.

Having a bath in the Tower –
Although there is no Mrs Durcan
For whom to leap out,

With whom to share
My room with a partial view –
(O Dearest Maeve Binchy,
Daredevil author of
A Room with a Partial View,
In Chicago in radio days
After a chat with Studs Terkel –
The dog's bollocks of chatters –
With Mary and Gordon
Being driven along LSD
In a white stretch limo
To stand in a soup line,
With Conor Cruise O'Brien,
The Prince of Haughtiness,
Tweedy, broken-veined,
Here many partial views
Of green groves, brown
Forests, blue mountains)
And Palestinian mothers
Running through gunfire
To the grocery store
On the corner – the corner
That is no more
(What a tragedy
If some cop it –
Cries Brother Tony Blair,
Whose precise lip
Reminds women in Labour
Of the Lord Adolf)
And in an Armani doorway

Orphan Monica –
Not on drink or drugs –
Wraps herself round
With Armani cardboard
For another night's sleep–
Lessness in the cold,
Cold Armani night,
And in Lecca a Moroccan man
With a bag of mud
Demands to be arrested
For drugs at the barracks
Of the carabinieri because
He is homeless,
I am praising the name
(For that's all I know of her)
Of the woman who made
This bathroom out of nothing
With its deep, deep bath
Freestanding on four squat
Legs, frescoed also
With pink lilies sprouting
Out of oceanic streams,
The cloud-perched herons
Stalking chimeras.
Her name is Beatrice.
Delighted to meet you,
Beatrice –
Beatrice Monti
della Corte von Rezzori.

Having a bath in the Tower –
Although there is no Mrs Durcan
To coo into my ear-trumpet
Soft sadistic soothings
Or to bring me champagne in bed
Or to plan holidays for us
In Madeira or Paris,
In Rapallo or Urbino,
And Uncle Colin Powell
Has gone home with his tail
Between his legs
(If in shuttle diplomacy
They have time
To powder their noses,
Why have they never the time
To give it their all?
Their terminal balls?
Their deathbed erections?)
And in Puglia near Brindisi
A pair of mother-and-son
Pit bull terriers have bitten
To death two farmhands –
I am praising the name
(For that's all I know of her)
Of the woman who made
This bathroom out of nothing,
Its miniature Art Deco
Toothbrush cabinet tacked
To the wall, an emerald-tinted
Two-door tin tabernacle

With two glass shelves;
Over bidet and lavatory
Its Art Deco wall light
Of scalloped delft.
Her name is Beatrice.
Delighted to meet you,
Beatrice –
Beatrice Monti
della Corte von Rezzori.

Having a bath in the Tower –
Although there is no Mrs Durcan
To answer the fax
Or to attend to the e-mail
Or to pay the bills
Or to do the big shopping
Or to hire or to fire
The servants – all of them
East European and
African, all of them
Shifting from foot to foot,
Not making eye contact
(Like Mary Magdalen and Mary
The Mother of God
In Piero's Arezzo
Fresco cycle)
And yesterday in France
Le Pen had a big success,
And one has to endure
Listening to self-righteous leftists

Beating their breasts
And whimpering and whingeing
And wailing at the walls
Of their own bathrooms
Feeling sorry for themselves –
The pure, yogurt-addicted,
Volvic-swilling, yoga-agitated
Robespierres of Paris,
Who never lift a finger
To do the washing up –
I am praising the name
(For that's all I know of her)
Of the woman who made
This bathroom out of nothing,
Facing west
To the mountains of Chianti,
Its one oval window
Which fills me with *skushno* –
That Russian word-installation
Of all that a child feels
In the bath alone, beseeching
The wall once and for all
To state if anything
Will ever change in this world,
This scarifying world,
And if Death be real.
Can Death be real?
No, Death is not real.
Death is a breeze-block.
Her name is Beatrice.

Delighted to meet you,
Beatrice –
Beatrice Monti
della Corte von Rezzori.

Having a bath in the Tower –
Although not having a Mrs Durcan
To conceal me in her skirts
Or in the ravines of her
Bosoms or in the forests
Of her hair or in the defiles
Of her thighs and to the world's
Press President Gerald Adams
From his Casa Blanca
In the Falls Road, Belfast,
Rejects the request to testify
Re the Colombia Three
In Washington before the House
Committee on International
Relations, but – President
Adams adds –
In that statesman's voice,
Mellifluous as it is malignant,
Intimate as it is intimidating –
That he'll permit legislators
To ask a few questions
Quote:
"Next time I'm in Washington"
Unquote
And the feature article

In today's *Corriere*
della Serra is headed
 "A Writer's Rendezvous
With Assassin's Bullet",
I am praising the name
(For that's all I know of her)
Of the woman who made
This bathroom out of nothing
With an Armenian mat
On polished bare floorboards
And the immersion
Heater whistling and
Grunting, the laundry basket
Of cream-white canvas
On slats that fold up
(A twentieth-century
Suburban Dublin
Pessimist could play
First-class cricket
In this bathroom)
Her name is Beatrice.
Delighted to meet you,
Beatrice —
Beatrice Monti
della Corte von Rezzori.

Having a bath in the Tower —
Although not having a Mrs Durcan
To be private with — Oh
What is a life with no

Privacy? It is not
Possible to be civilised
Without having a woman
To be private with. How
Tired I am of being
A fifty-seven-year old public,
Affable, absentminded ass,
And in Paris the middle-aged
Right and Left
Are deodorizing their armpits
And their dimpled chins
In preparation for May Day –
Le Pen would adore
Riots, bloodshed
And the French Left
Is so narcissistic as to
Maybe grant him his wish,
And here in the convent
Of Santa Maddalena
The Tuscan housekeeper
With a beehive in her hair
Is taunting and needling
The Albanian cook,
Whose delicious smile
Out-minestrone's
Michelangelo's minestrone,
I am praising the name
(For that's all I know of her)
Of the woman who made
This bathroom out of nothing

With its *silenzio profondo*,
In spite of which
A photograph was taken
Of Saint Edmund White
In the bathtub at prayer,
An open book for a fig-leaf,
(Published in *Vanity Fair*)
And the door also squeaks
Fiesta!
Siesta!
Basta!
And the flush in the lavatory
Works like Garibaldi
Having an orgasm –
And so we are all born
Into the baths of injustice.
Her name is Beatrice.
Delighted to meet you,
Beatrice –
Beatrice Monti
della Corte von Rezzori.

Having a bath in the Tower –
Although not having a George
To Butler me –
I am as hypochondriacal
As Raphaelo of Donnini,
And Brina the Slovenian
Workers' Party Princess
Is keen to advise me

Daily and kindly
About my alimentation,
My incorrect diet,
My all-too-mentionable defects –
He does not cook,
He does not drive,
He does not drink –
And Dennis Bock
Of Hungary and Toronto,
Never slow to deflate
His inflationary colleagues,
Asking me why
I close doors,
Why not leave doors open?
Asks he not unreasonably,
I am homesick for Ireland,
Yet sicker at having
To return to Ireland,
Where woods are waste lands
For young farmers to roar around
In four-wheel drives, felling
Every tree in sight,
Ancient beech, oak,
The older the better;
Ireland where art
And imagination
Have been substituted
By Thatcherism and despair –
Father Kavanagh dying
By the roadside,

Brother Hartnett dying
By another roadside,
Mother Yeats atop
Her hollow nest —
I am praising the name
(For that's all I know of her)
Of the woman who made
This bathroom out of nothing,
Its mirror whose eloquence
Is silence — the bearded silence
Of a David Sylvester
After having been asked
A question — a silence
Of bears in conclave.
Who shall we elect
As the next great
First mate?
Her name is Beatrice.
Delighted to meet you,
Beatrice —
Beatrice Monti
della Corte von Rezzori.

Having a bath in the Tower —
Although not having a Kitty
To Patrick my gravity —
I am happy as Nayla
From Romania, but living
In Amsterdam pregnant
With her second child,

Nayla whose dad hails
From the Sudan, her mum
Alive and well in Romania,
Transylvania in the Carpathians,
Dearest Nayla Mohamed Elamin Habiballa
Abu El Maali Cocea Manolescu Pincas,
To Ireland I have to go back
To my mother in the nursing home,
Progressing with Alzheimers.
How is it possible any more
To speak of the Great Memory?
My shagged mother!
She who for fifteen years
Raged against old age –
I am eighty-four – enough! –
Only to be festooned
With Dementia's
Crenellated paper hat,
Its drooling bib.
What use to her now
Her Christian plummet?
What to measure?
Does the imagination
Dwell the most
Upon a commode won
Or a commode lost?
Does the imagination dwell
In the Rape-house of Memory?
The imagination by definition
Does not dwell, period.

By definition the imagination
Is itinerant, transient,
Necessarily, dutifully,
Serenading excretion, stop.
My mother clings
To her empty handbag,
A little black leather yoke of a thing
With a very long shoulder strap,
So, so unfashionable.
Women should know that handbags
Should never have straps –
Advises Celia Larkin
In the sunny south-east,
Kellys of Rosslare;
Women should never wear brooches
On their lapels, women should never
Expose their breast bones.
Joseph I. Cornell counter-advises:
Women should wear, wear, wear.
Imagination not born
Of its occasion
Is a put-on, and boring.
I am praising the name
(For that's all I know of her)
Of the woman who made
This bathroom out of nothing,
Its stacks of dog-eared *Spectator*s
Waiting to be reread
Under its heyday editorship
Of Alexander Chancellor –

An Englishman who at luncheon
Gazing over at you myopically
Speaks *sotto voce* of a woman
"Who met a Captain Boxer in China";
Than whom there is no
Editor more fluently,
Candidly, flagrantly
Dedicated to the ephemeral.
Her name is Beatrice.
Delighted to meet you,
Beatrice –
Beatrice Monti
della Corte von Rezzori.

Not having a bath in the Tower –
But having once had a Mrs Durcan
Twenty Botticelli years ago
And blown it, and
Sunk to the sea's bottom,
To the crab-infested nadir
Of a drowned submarine
Inside a vodka bottle,
Cool, coolly
The nightmare raves on,
An aged, necessitous,
Devout poet
In the gateway stands,
A computer in his hands
Trailing flex and leads,
The camp guards –

All-American boys –
Prod him, flail him,
Rifle butts, boots, and
Last night at Ponte Canale
Near Terni the bungee jump
Of a young couple – Alberto
And Tiziana – "went wrong"
(But the video did not go wrong)
And Israeli Defence Force
Snipers are shooting
Into the Church of the Nativity
In Bethlehem – Oh
Why does not the Pope
Helicopter
Into Bethlehem himself –
Oh where is the soul
Of St Thomas à Becket –
(Poet's imaginings?
Realist's thinkings?)
I am as unhappy, but resigned
As Volker Schlondorf
Having to sell his house.
How it all comes down
In the end to land!
(To hold land not ours
We invent religion.)
I am praising the name
(For that's all I know of her)
Of the woman who made
This bathroom out of nothing

With its towel rack
In the twilight empty
And a man overflowing with meaning
Doing his best to obey
The word of that woman,
A wild female pilgrim
With a pug in her scrip
Whose mission on earth
Is to make people at home.
Her name is Beatrice.
Delighted to meet you,
Beatrice —
Beatrice Monti
della Corte von Rezzori.

III

Nature is enough or should be.
After Nature we should lie down and die
Noiselessly as we can, without self-pity,
Rodomontade, cant, justification.
There is around the tower at its base
Instead of smug, pestiferous sycophants
And the murdering faces of TV and press
A garden enclosed, a *hortus conclusus*
In which we may or may not conclude
Our war, our famine, our migration.
Top of the tower to you!
Now Gregor von Rezzori it is time:
Go walk the plank without a blindfold

To disappear inside the porphyry–apostrophe'd
Sandstone pyramid of time.
Your ashes stroll, speck by speck,
Up the tamarisk steps to your burial place
Under the three lindens,
In the distance your last and original home
Bubbling in violet wistaria,
Golden Banksia rose,
And the Great Peony of Santa Maddalena
Swallows up a great man's greater wife.
All is dedicated to the necessity of life.

30 April 2002

Alitalia Flight 295 Dublin–Milan

About to board the flight for Italy,
Do not buy the biography of Primo Levi.

Let there be an end to biography:
Biography is lechery.

If you want to know Primo Levi,
Read the poetry of Primo Levi.

The poetry is the story:
The story is the life.

Santa Maddalena

in memoriam Bruce Chatwin

I find myself lost somewhere between
Poggibonsi and Pontassieve,
But Mohammed drives to my rescue.
He takes me to Donnini where I find sanctuary
With Signor and the Baronessa von Rezzori.
Next day he purchases me a traveller's alarm clock
In a blue and black case with a white face.
Mohammed is lean and lurky and, when
He smiles, the gridlock on the autostrada
Abates, and I am not afraid in the night
To be a back-seat passenger in a white Honda Civic
Or to be alone in water at my life's conclusion.
In this same bathtub many have soaked
And all were chosen.

The Art of Life

A young French family's meanderings
On the cobblestones between the wings
Of the Uffizi Gallery in Florence,
Between the lines of pavement artists
Marketing watercolours of the Ponte Vecchio
Or instant portraiture,
Converge on, circle, halt,
Hover at the stall announcing
Caricatura 10 Euro.

In a card-table chair, a man in black
With silver highlights in his black hair,
Black wraparound Ray-Ban sunglasses,
Long nose hooked over thick-lipped mouth,
Laconically dragging on a cigarette,
Legs crossed at the knees.
Slouching in inscrutability
He could be a casual wife-beater
Or a safe, devoted father.

The yellow-shirted ten-year-old son
Clamours to have his caricature done.
Papa hesitates (as papas do),
But Maman immediately acquiesces.
When the question is her unique son

A mother will always trumpet
Where a father fears to coo.
Yet not even she on her decisive feet
Foresees the repercussions.

The appallingly blank cartridge paper –
The white suspense of nothing happening –
The forensic silence of calculation –
The first probings of the scalpel-nibbed pen –
The first smudges of the charcoal –
The awakening of the laid-back artist –
The emergence of a hairline
Decipherable as her unique son –
The unbelievable rebirth of his laughing soul.

The portrait done, the artist allows
A smile to kindle the clouds of his face.
He holds up the portrait for all to see.
Passers-by cluster round the happy birth.
High in the east wing of the Uffizi
The head of a curator peers out of a window.
Papa looks over at his wife and blushes,
Just as he did ten years ago
In the maternity hospital in Nancy.

And she – Mama – *Mère* – *Maman* –
She is bashfuller than Mary
In a triptych of the Annunciation
And prouder by a nostril's gauntlet –
Her newborn son alighting on earth

Under the noses of Giotto and Dante.
She lets out a snorted scream,
The scones and jam of her being
Hot on the stones of Tuscany.

Report to Rezzori

Chernopol 13 May 1914 – Donnini 23 April 1998

For three weeks I have been sitting on the wrought-iron
bench at the stone table in the grove of your linden trees
listening out for you.

What I hear is the tick-tock of the grandfather clock of your
gratitude to your Beatrice,
who after your wanderlust years – few of them fun – gave
you and made you a nest in the valley of the Arno where
you could feel at home, and did, and do, for a night or
two.

Through the uproarious street-life of birds at their feeding
and shopping, I hear your voice calling me from a nearby
café called The Pyramid where, at a wine-red porphyry
tabletop, you sit scribbling in your tattered notebook.

Impatient, but smiling you cry: *There is only one essential thing
and that is to be polite, not smart.*

The day before yesterday, Sunday, the 4th Sunday after Easter,
Le Pen had a big success in France and the one-eyed left-
wing conscience is wailing and swotting the air with
rolled-up copies of *Le Monde* and *Libération*. Child of the

Bukovina, excoriator of self-pity and hysteria and self-righteousness and penny-pinching and nostalgia, you laugh that hunter's laugh of yours: *Not a capercaillie in sight! It's* skushno *on the hoof all right!*

Rezzori, only men of no party like you know how to light a fire from the ashes of the night. Cheers.

Aldeburgh October Storm

At noon at reception in the small, sedate, family-run
Wentworth Hotel in Aldeburgh
Such are the numbers of guests trooping in the door in gusts
and windfalls
I find I can neither check in or check out, but instead shel-
ter in a corner
Watching the jostling and cries and stumbles and embraces
and handshakes and pecks and ejaculations.
There are two parties commencing simultaneously – the
landlord tells me,
His pinstripe shirtsleeves rolled up, his silk yellow tie unfurl-
ing over his left shoulder:
In the conservatory the christening party of the first son of
the Briggs-Palmers, Jonny,
Named after the English international rugby outhalf, Jonny
Wilkinson
And in the library Lady Stevenson-Ellis's ninetieth birthday
party,
Lady Florence Stevenson-Ellis of Grundisburgh.
All the guests have got mixed up in the foyer
And what with the bedlam and the wild wet balmy gale
blowing in every time the door opens,
The wheelchairs are winding up at the christening party, while
The go-carts are shooting around Lady Stevenson-Ellis's
ankles

And there's not a thing she can do about it, but she doesn't
     mind –
She survived the Normandy landings and she still has not got
     Parkinson's –
Shouts General Fairley-Duff, himself shaking all over,
To which General McMillan-Thorpe shouts:
"Is there anyone here who has not got Parkinson's?"
Where have I seen all this before?
Ah yes – at Becher's Brook first time round, all sixty-seven
     horses
Taking off together, leaping together, landing together, falling
     together, getting up together.
Who ever said the English nation is dead? Or that the English
     nation has lost its soul?
Preponderance of leaf in sunlight in storm – is what I say.
In the face of grief we put our best foot forward, crimson and
     gold in the face of grief.
Hey-ho, trample my shingle, but if it isn't Ingrid Eason over
     there,
Knew her when she was a Wren, one of the Easons of
     Dublin, newsagents.
Well, what does it matter so long as it pays the mortgage off,
     a net earner,
And, don't look but that's Edwin de Vere Todd, lovely bloke,
     used work for me, utterly useless, totally amoral, King's Lynn;
Only this morning I was feeling doggone abysmal, Jack, – oh
     God I do want to sit down, upholstery or wicker, Jack? –
But I said to myself: come on, old boy, get out your best
     hounds-tooth

And your best twill and take down your blackthorn stick
   and
So here I am, a large G and T in hand, and still not sure
   whether I'm at the Briggs-Palmer christening
Or at Lady Stevenson-Ellis's ninetieth. By Jove, *some* day, isn't
   it, *some* rain, but warm rain, eh?
Seagulls all over the shop, seagulls as big as frankfurters on
   stilts, big as frigging Viking longships.
See the lifeboat beetling out this morning?
And the North Sea behaving more like the darned Atlantic
   than the North Sea?
Some bloody Norwegian trawler no doubt.
How is, tell me, it's always us that's rescuing them, eh?
Anyway cheers, and let's hope young Briggs-Palmer is half
   the man Lady Stevenson-Ellis has been –
Well, you know what I mean! Come on, old girl, don't be
   an old stick in the mud!
We'll all beat this Parkinson's, if I've any say in the matter,
Suffolk is the best place in the world – at least I think it is,
Even if life is all Dutch to us lot, and Aldeburgh's the peach
   in the orchard,
Yesterday I had to step over a chap in Neptune Alley, what
Are drunkards coming to at all these days, I says to myself,
Another large G and T there, my good man, and a smear of
   that black caviar on a cheese-stick wouldn't be a bad idea,
Excuse me ma'am, we English, you know, we may be down
   on our luck, but we do bring a bit of malarkey into this
   old black kip of a world, don't we?
Madam, I do beg your pardon.

The Old Man and the Conference

The third morning of the conference,
The Warsaw World Social Studies Conference,
Sitting down at a vacant table
To wallow in a silent, solitary breakfast,
I saw a small, old man
Heading for my table and heard him say
"May I join you?"
I smiled "Yes, of course."
But popping a slice of kiwi fruit into my mouth
I cursed him.
He asked me if I would mind clarifying for him
A remark in my lecture of the previous day
Comparing the Catholic Church in Ireland in the 1950s
To the Communist Party in Poland in the 1950s.
"Scrambled egg," he laughed, pointing down at his plate.
Accelerating backwards into the cul-de-sac of his enthusiasm
I was so surprised by his eyes –
Their youthfulness under his tiny, bald head –
I almost crashed into the lamp-post of his innocence.
At that instant I noticed a small silver brooch
In the left lapel of his blue blazer
Comprising two italicised letters – *AK*.
AK! I am sitting opposite a man who fought
In the Warsaw Uprising in 1944

When the *AK* – the Home Army of the Polish Government
     in exile –
Rose up against the Nazis, but were destroyed,
While on the far bank of the River Vistula
The Soviet Army – the Red Liberator –
Sat back, not lifting a rifle to help.
The old man with the child's eyes –
A man with no ego –
Tells me that all he remembers of the Warsaw Uprising
Is one day near the end when fighting in a house
On the ground floor or the basement,
He cannot remember which,
Amid gunfire and shelling,
He looked up and saw dangling from a banister
A woman's leg. He looks over at me
Across a plate of scrambled egg and a bowl of kiwi fruit
And he looks up at the ceiling and I look up with him:
"A woman's leg in a nylon stocking and, I think,
Yes, I am sure, a shoe."
He was taken prisoner by the Nazis and taken to Germany.
After the war he spent two years in New York
Doing a thesis in Fordham University.
He wanted to remain in New York, but returned to Poland
Because he was an only child and he feared also
The other repercussions on his father and mother.
His thesis was entitled "The Early Novels of Ernest
     Hemingway".

A Poet in Poland

to Anthony Cronin

On Tuesday the 21st of October 2003
In a sixth-storey classroom in a university in central Poland
A poet born in 1925 in the south-east of Ireland
Circles to his feet, stands at the bar
Before the crammed-into-a-tin-can faces of students sitting,
    crouching, squatting, standing,
Their medieval iconic faces hieratic, open-eyed,
And he shakes out his years – seventy-eight years – from his
    eyebrows and shoulders
Like a swan shaking out the water from his neck-fleece and
    wing-feathers
And opening his mouth, he closes his mouth.
Is he smiling or weeping?

A poet who has tramped here by way of four airports and
    two railway stations
In Ireland, England, Poland,
Under a tall-stemmed angle-poise lamp
He holds up his book in his hands three inches from his
    eyes;
He begins to read aloud in an elegiac, laconic, heraldic voice.

Between stanzas I glance up at him
And I catch a glimpse of the holy mountain of his head –
The Mont Sainte-Victoire of his head.
A bare, conical head; a tree; a blackboard.
The engrossment of the students is echoing his voice;
Closer and closer they are leaning forwards and they also
Have become part of the quartz cone of his holy head
As pilgrims they ascend all together with satchel and scrip.

From far off across the wide river Pripyat – from across the
    smoking fires of the Pripyat marshes,
Whence all our Slav mothers and our Slav fathers came –
In the night sky I see a ziggurat of head-torches
Spiralling upwards around and around his cranium
And we are all alpinists as well as pilgrims of his cranium
And we are not deterred by altitude sickness
From going on with him to the summit of his poem
Up above the death-zone at 29, 000 feet
And as he utters the last lines of his poem –
A poem entitled "The End of the Modern World" –
We are all perched on the peak of his bare head – only
I am standing the far side of passport control and he
He is swaying into it, his torso and legs going one way,
His head going another way, his bottle-glass spectacles askew,
But he has passport in hand and he is slouching through
The towers of Poznan and Warsaw
Silent, astonishing and new.

The Holy Cross, Warsaw

to Leland Bardwell

It was a sub-zero, sun-scalded morning in down-town
  Warsaw
And I was lost and the car was leaving in an half an hour.
I ran in to a church off the street – up steps through three
  doors –
It was like running into the sea. I fell –
I nearly fell – I half-fell – I fell to my knees –
My head bouncing sideways. Such masses of people.
Not at Mass. Not at Benediction. Not at anything.
Not old people only. All ages. All staring.
In silence. Staring into space. At all angles
From one another. Staring at walls. Staring out of walls.
Like bathers on a bank-holiday weekend all together
Getting into the water at the same time, yet of course not.
Like people getting married every minute all over the world.
Or getting shot. Or getting born. All of it. Out of. Into. At.
  Will.
And the silence so absolute which seems improbable
In a down-town city street in Warsaw on a Friday morning
But it was just so. So silent, so still.

From out of my millennia of skull
In all of that silent stillness,

From out of my eye-craters,
I pluck a – I pick a – splinter floating
Free of the emotion (no longer trapped,
No longer a fossil of false gods)
Inexorably being cue-balled downstream.

I climb to my feet and I am running out the doors.
At the bottom of the steps I trip over an infant
In pink swaddling clothes – only she isn't an infant –
She's a very old, agèd, ancient lady the size of an infant,
Strewn on the footpath with a knitted pink cap on her skull
And I stop and I stare and as I nudge a few złotys into her
    cup
I see that her eyeballs are peeling bald – she
Has so many, that many cataracts – I turn away in a fright
Only to catch a glimpse in the vertical sky of the Stalin
    Towers
Of the Palace of Culture and Science,
Where the car will be leaving from Warsaw Central –
I am running along Novy Swiat, running
Across empty allotments of clothes lines,
My head getting snarled up again and again in double white
    sheets,
The car oh the car – I am climbing into the back seat
Under the Stalin Towers – all that Manhattan Venetian
    Gothic Art Deco of some fundamentalist pre-Christian
    deity, is that what twentieth-century collective corporate
    man was? –
And I am being driven at speed to the airport
Downstream, a splinter in a red anorak, past

Massed graves of golden leaves,
Oh all the women in my life I betrayed,
All of them with their backs turned to me,
Planting trees wherever they may be,
Making sandcastles for their children's children,
After wars we always plant trees,
After wars we always make sandcastles,
The driver chatting to the dispatcher about someone called
  Monika.
After check-in – "she knew we were coming" –
"The hand of you-know-who" –
Next flight to Moskva at 4.30 p.m. –
I hear people talking yet again about the Polish Pope –
Karol Wojtyla – how ill he really is now, how seriously ill –
And that 1966 poem of his called "Easter Vigil" –
And an eighty-year-old woman with the gait of a teenager
And with a blue rucksack on her back,
Grinning out of long grey curls, starts talking about Knock
And about Monsignor Horan of Knock and how he had said
In Lourdes not in Knock, as forwards falling he flung himself
  under his cross:
"I'm an old man in a hurry and I've a long way to go"
To the Church of the Holy Cross in Warsaw.

Tarnowo Podgorne

6.30 a.m. in a roadhouse in Tarnowo Podgorne
About halfway between Warsaw and Berlin,
Lining up at the counter, a man and woman ask me
"Are you from Dublin? So are we.
What are you doing in Tarnowo Podgorne?
A poetry reading, is it?"
Marian is wearing a blue Dublin Fire Brigade shirt.
Rory is wearing a blue City of New York Fire Brigade shirt.
"We've got a transit van packed with stuff
For children in the Belorussian orphanages.
The sort of things we take for granted in Dublin –
Women's sanitaries, soap dispensers, Sudo cream –
Things you'd never think of –
And a transport incubator that we got from Holles Street.
Good luck with your poetry reading in Tarnowo Podgorne –
We're hoping to make it to Minsk tonight."

Wild Sports of Japan

to Mamoru Odajima and Michiko Wakamatsu

That snow-bound January we spent
Shooting motor cars in northern Japan
In one short afternoon
I bagged five Mitsubishi and one Nissan.

The Incontinence of Fame

The man with the eagle eye is not a celebrity;
Eagles do not excrete in their own nests.

Civilisations

If I were Japanese
I'd wear silk,
Rouge and ashes,
And under the cherry trees
All day long I'd smirk.

6.30 a.m., 13 January 2004, Hokkaido Prefecture

Human beings are peculiar creatures which is why we
    cranes –
We red-crested Japanese cranes –
Congregate at daybreak in the shallow bend of the river
To shoot video of human beings on the red bridge.

The Jerusalem–Tokyo Fault Line

The Buddhist monks in the temple at Takahatafudo
Are the only impolite people I have met in Japan:
Like the Jewish clerics at the Wailing Wall
Their prime concern, their only concern
Is the extraction of cash from the innocent pilgrim.

Raftery in Tokyo

Suicidal in Tokyo,
A crow on a telegraph pole
Raucous with self-pity,
Ah, ah, ah – I squawk.

From County Mayo to Greater Tokyo
Men with failing eyesight go
Serenading that crazy innocence
They see because they know.

On the Road to the Airport

The most terrible person I ever met was my father.
Only my mother was occasionally not terrible.
Terrible terrible
Was my father;
Terribler than Mao.
But now in my own old age
On the road to the airport –
Serious snow –
I do not need to know,
I do not need to meet
Any more of the terrible people.
So, father, father,
Stand clear of my stuttering propellers,
Stand clear of my blistered feet,
Stand clear of my ring-less fingers,
Stand clear of my red eyes.

The Journey Home from Japan

The hard part of the journey home
To Ireland from Japan
Is not the fourteen hours in the air
Nor the bumps in the ceilings
Between Mongolia and Siberia
Nor when over Norway the pilot drawls
"Boys and girls – glad you're still with us"
Nor the maze of Heathrow
Nor the rat-run of the London-Dublin flight
Nor the cave-light of Dublin Airport.
The hard part,
Having stumbled from the taxi
And fumbled with the key in the door,
Is facing into my place
Smelling of droppings of suicide.
At least back in Japan
Suicide is an honourable end,
Not like in Ireland
A furtive act of disgrace.

Checkout Girl

A week back in Ireland from Japan,
But I cannot stop bowing.
Only ten minutes ago in the supermarket
I bowed to the checkout girl
With the red cheeks and the limp.

I bowed from the waist to her
And she blushed and I think
When she limps home this afternoon,
Collecting her toddler from the crèche,
It may be with an extra spring in her limp.

Facing Extinction

to Masazumi Toraiwa

When I rounded the corner into Anne Street
And I was confronted by a man squatting in a doorway
I got a shock and I flinched.
For the face I saw was the same face
I saw in the shaving mirror this morning.
Dropping my ludicrous lucre into his beaker
I squeaked: "Are you all right?"
He announced: "I think I'm going to be all right."
And he proffered me a smile, looking me straight in the eye.

I crossed over into Chatham Street
And I slipped into The Great Outdoors
Where I purchased a pair of walking shoes –
Brasher Hillmasters –
Having been instructed last week in northern Hokkaido
By a samurai-ninja protector of bears –
Brown bears facing extinction –
That the time was nigh
For me to face the truth about my fellow creatures.

On my way back along Anne Street
There was a different man in the same doorway
Looking more doomed than the first man –
More doomed to extinction –

His head bowed as if in meditation on death.
Dropping my ludicrous lucre into his beaker
I squeaked: "Are you all right?"
He announced: "I'm fine – how are you?"
And he proffered me a smile, looking me straight in the eye.

In my cave on the edge of the city
A woman on the telephone mocks me:
"You were always a bear"
As if I *should/could* have been somebody else.
Peering again into my shaving mirror
At my bear's eyes, my bear's mouth,
I am surprised by how upbeat, yet melancholy, I look:
In the autumn of my days I am looking forward
To hibernation, facing extinction.